INSPIRATION

For Your

JOURNEY

~ 40 ~
Daily Devotionals

INSPIRATION

For Your

JOURNEY

~ 40 ~

Daily Devotionals

NICOLE E. JOHNSON

REDEMPTION
PRESS

Published by Redemption Press, PO Box 427, Enumclaw, WA 98022

Toll Free (844) 2REDEEM (273-3336)

Redemption Press is honored to present this title in partnership with the author. The views expressed or implied in this work are those of the author. Redemption Press provides our imprint seal representing design excellence, creative content, and high quality production.

Unless otherwise noted, all Scripture references are taken from the New King James Version®. Copyright © 1982 by Thomas Nelson. Used by permission. All rights reserved.

Scripture quotations marked KJV are taken from the Holy Bible, King James Version, © 1979, 1980, 1982 by Thomas Nelson, Inc., Publishers. Used by permission.

Scripture quotations marked AMP are taken from the Amplified Bible, Copyright © 1954, 1958, 1962, 1964, 1965, 1987 by The Lockman Foundation. Used by permission.

Scripture quotations marked NLT are taken from the Holy Bible, New Living Translation, copyright © 1996, 2004, 2015 by Tyndale House Foundation. Used by permission of Tyndale House Publishers Inc., Carol Stream, Illinois 60188. All rights reserved.

Scripture quotations marked NIV are taken from the Holy Bible, New International Version®, NIV® Copyright ©1973, 1978, 1984, 2011 by Biblica, Inc.® Used by permission. All rights reserved worldwide.

ISBN: 978-1-68314-595-0 (Paperback)
978-1-68314-596-7 (Hard Cover)
978-1-68314-597-4 (ePub)
978-1-68314-598-1 (Mobi)

Library of Congress Catalog Card Number: 2018949412

Dedication

This book is dedicated to Gail Clarke Johnson, my mother, my best friend, my inspiration, my quiet strength, and my guardian angel. I love you, and may you enjoy heaven as you sleep in peace, my sweet angel!

Contents

Acknowledgments

Thank You, God, for this amazing life journey, and thank You, Holy Spirit, for inspiring me to write this book. I would like to give a big thank you to my dad, Eugene Johnson Sr., for being one of my biggest supporters and fans. Thanks to my brothers, Eugene and Gary, for their continued love and support. Finally, I would like to thank all of my family, supporters, and readers for believing in the vision God has given me.

Introduction

Dear reader,

This devotional was birthed out of my life experiences over the last several years.

As I have traveled this spiritual journey and process, I chronicled words of motivation as well as inspiration through Scripture and prayer. After reflecting upon my journal and through the sharing of my experiences with family and friends, I was encouraged to share these times of reflection. This devotional is the summation of the Scriptures and prayers that guided me and gave me strength in some of the most challenging seasons of my life.

There are forty days of inspirational devotionals in this book. Each chapter is designed with the intention to inspire and renew vital parts of your existence. You will find devotionals on love, peace, comfort, encouragement, wisdom, faith, and patience. I hope you will be inspired, encouraged, and blessed by each Scripture and prayer as much as I have been. Please read this book often. It will inspire you while on your journey.

Nicole E. Johnson, BSN, MBA

You Are Loved

Keep me as the apple of Your eye; hide me under
the shadow of Your wings. (Psalm 17:8)

My earthly father always tells me that I am the
apple of his eye. His words give me such comfort. How
much more does my heavenly Father consider me the
apple of His eye?

If you haven't had a good relationship with your
earthly father, it may be hard for you to see yourself as
the apple of God's eye. Maybe negative tapes of unkind
words spoken during your childhood still ring in your
ears.

Remember, despite what anyone else has said, you
are the apple of God's eye and He loves you. You are
fearfully and wonderfully made in His image.

So the next time you have feelings of worthlessness
or insignificance, please remember you are special to
God. He takes great delight in you, and you have great

value in His eyes. Why? you may ask. He loves you because He made you. You were created in His image and His likeness. He is the lover of your soul, so you are the apple of His eye. Receive the love of Christ today.

Tip of the Day: You are valuable, and you are loved by God.

Prayer: *Lord,* Your Word tells me that I am made in Your image and likeness. I am fearfully and wonderfully made by You. When I feel less than valuable or like I have been forgotten, help me to remember Your great love for me. I am, indeed, the apple of your eye. Thanks for Your unwavering and unconditional love for me. I am blessed. In Jesus's name I pray. Amen.

....

....

....

....

....

....

....

....

....

....

....

....

....

....

....

....

....

....

....

❧ DAY 2 ❧

Faithful

> The Lord always keeps his promises; he is gracious in
> all he does. The Lord helps the fallen and lifts those
> bent beneath their loads. (Psalm 145:13–14 NLT)

God is faithful and completely dependable, no
matter what things look like through our eyes. Sometimes we doubt if the promises of God will come to
pass in our lives due to crisis, difficult situations, major
delays, death, loss, and mistakes that are made. However, we have to remember that God wants to see us ac-
complishing *His* ultimate goals, purposes, and destiny
for our lives. He wants us to walk into that which *He*
has promised us.

Today, I am reminded of the "Hall of Faith" found
in Hebrews 11. God gave Abraham and Sarah their
promised son. He made David a king in spite of his
faults and mistakes. He parted the Red Sea so the Isra-
elites could escape the Egyptians. He preserved Noah

and his family's lives during the flood and did much more.

None of these things occurred without those involved experiencing challenges or adversity. However, I am encouraged that just as God saw all of these individuals through, He can and will do the same for us. God sent His Holy Spirit to be our helper, our compass in life, and our Comforter. Sometimes we go through difficult times, hardships, and delays, yet we see that God *always* fulfills *His* promises. The answers may not come when and how we want them, but God honors His promises to us.

In this season, let's purpose to walk by faith and not by sight. This is easier said than done. However, we can trust God at His Word, knowing He has never failed us yet!

Tip of the Day: Trust Him to do what He said He would do in your life. He won't fail you.

Prayer: *Lord,* thank You for Your Word, for in it I find all truth. You are faithful, and I have seen the evidence in my life. Forgive me for ever doubting You. Help me to trust You more. In Jesus's name I pray. Amen.

....

....

....

....

....

....

....

....

....

....

....

....

....

....

INSPIRATION FOR YOUR JOURNEY

....

....

....

....

....

....

....

....

....

....

....

....

....

❧ DAY 3 ❧

Faith and Endurance

My brethren, count it all joy when you fall into various trials, knowing that the testing of your faith produces patience. But let patience have *its* perfect work, that you may be perfect and complete, lacking nothing. If any of you lacks wisdom, let him ask of God, who gives to all liberally and without reproach, and it will be given to him. (James 1:2–5)

All of us have experienced pain in our lives. It can come from a number of things: death of a loved one, broken relationships, termination from a job, or divorce. Sometimes God allows pain as part of a process for leading us to our purpose, which oftentimes will propel us to destiny.

James 1:2–3 says it like this: "When troubles of any kind come your way, consider it an opportunity for great joy. For you know that when your faith is tested, your endurance has a chance to grow" (NLT). This is so powerful and profound to me. When trials come my way, I can consider it an opportunity for great joy! It seems like an oxymoron. However, when I ponder the thought, it makes sense.

When our faith is being tested, our endurance has an opportunity to grow. In the process of enduring, we usually learn things about ourselves that we didn't know before. We learn how to be vulnerable. We learn how to rebound. We develop perseverance and resilience and learn that we will survive. In the end, we see that what the enemy meant for bad God turned around for our good. On the other side of pain comes victory.

So the next time you go through a trial, decide in your mind that it is an opportunity to allow God to walk you through it. While stretching your faith, He will allow you to learn how much you can endure through Him, and how His strength is made perfect in weakness. He will lead you to a victorious end.

Tip of the Day: When facing a trial, rely on God for help, comfort, wisdom, and the ability to endure.

Prayer: *Lord,* I stand in need of Your help and strength today. Help me to remember that You are always there for me in my time of need. As I seek You in this situation, I ask for Your guidance and wisdom. Help me to remember to count it all joy when I face various trials, knowing that it is working in me greater faith, patience, and endurance. Hallelujah! I thank You that I can rest, knowing that You are working things out on my behalf so there will be nothing lacking, and that the end of my test and trial will result in victory through You. I pray this In Jesus's name. Amen.

....

....

....

....

....

....

....

....

....

....

....

....

....

....

....

....

....

....

....

....

....

....

⤳ **DAY 4** ⤶

Stay Focused and Get Busy

Being confident of this very thing, that He who has begun a good work in you will complete *it* until the day of Jesus Christ. (Philippians 1:6)

No matter where we are on our journeys or what we are going through, God has promised to complete the work He started in our lives. Many of us have experienced loss, setbacks, disappointments, and delays. The enemy would love to use such things to kill, steal, and destroy our visions, passions, dreams, and purposes.

When he goes on the attack, our natural response is to get discouraged, dismayed, or distracted. But this is when we most need to stay focused and continue to move forward. When we pray, press, and proceed forward with passion, fulfilling our purposes, we discover that we can do anything that God has ordained for us to do. The key is remembering the good news and the truth of God's Word. All things are possible to those who believe. All things *are possible* through Christ Jesus. Now that's encouraging! The world is waiting for *what you have to offer.* Ask God to help you see the possibilities that await *you.*

Tip of the Day: God is still working in your life. Don't give up!

Prayer: *Lord,* I'm thankful that with You, endless possibilities await me. You have already laid out the plan for my life. Help me to slow down, listen for Your instructions, and walk them out obediently. I trust You, Lord. Thank You for giving me dreams, vision, and purpose. Help me to walk out and fulfill what You have called me to do. Help me to be salt to the earth, light to the world, a disciple of Your Word, and an ambassador for Your kingdom. In Jesus's name I pray. Amen.

....

....

....

....

....

....

....

....

....

....

....

....

....

....

....

....

....

....

....

....

....

....

....

....

....

....

....

~ DAY 5 ~

God's Greater Plan

Many are the plans in a person's heart, but it is the Lord's purpose that prevails. (Proverbs 19:21 NIV)

There are times when I question whether or not God sees what is going on in my life. It seems like His promises for my life will never come to pass. I must remember, however, that the plans He has for His children stand forever. His plans are often far different and much better than ours. His thoughts are not always our thoughts. He doesn't always do things the way we would. His timing is certainly not always in line with ours.

It helps to remember that God's plans for us are great. His intentions toward us never change. Most of all, His love for us is unwavering. People change, circumstances change, jobs change, and relationships change.

When you find yourself wondering what the future holds or if anything positive will come out of the journey you're on, know that you can trust God. Jeremiah 29:11 in The Message Bible says, "I'll show up and take care of you as I promise . . . I know what I'm doing. I have it all planned out—plans to take care of you, not abandon you, plans to give you the future you hope for."

God's Word consistently reminds us that the plans of His heart stand forever from generation to generation. God has your back!

Tip of the Day: Remember that God's plans for you are far better than the ones you have for yourself. Trust Him.

Prayer: *God*, thank You that when all else changes, You remain the same. Help me remember to trust, not in what I see, but in the faith I have in You. You, indeed, have my life in Your hands. Thank You that Your promises for me are yes and amen. My future is safe and secure with You. Help me to walk the road that You have paved for me with faith and love, knowing that Your expected end for me is great. I pray all this in Jesus's name. Amen!

....

....

....

....

....

....

....

....

....

....

....

....

....

....

....

....

....

....

....

....

....

....

....

....

....

....

....

....

DAY 6

Write the Vision and Run with It

Where there is no vision, the people perish: but he that keepeth the law, happy is he. (Proverbs 29:18 KJV)

Is there something you have always wanted to accomplish but it has yet to come to pass? Maybe you've wanted to become an author, start your own business, make a career change, get married, have children, or just live a more balanced life. Whatever it is, you can do it! Write out your dreams and visions. Put them in a place where you can see them daily. Believe that it can happen! Surround yourself with people who are doing what you want to do and will motivate you to get going.

The author and inspirational entrepreneur Lisa Nichols said it best when she stated, "Don't ever wait until it is perfect because you will never start!"

I have learned that it is important to reflect on our past, build on our positive experiences, and learn from our mistakes. Obviously, we don't want to live in the past or reflect on it for so long that we get stuck in that place. We need to be present and sober in the present time. We must also be careful not to be in such a hurry to get to the next thing that we don't take time to smell the roses and glean from our rich experiences, both good or bad.

It helps to be grateful for life and the chance to do whatever has been placed in our heart to do. We can look toward the future and purpose within ourselves to live our best life ever and to live it more abundantly. Make your declaration to live out your dreams and walk out visions. Pray over everything and give thanks in all things. You are a winner! You are a conqueror! You are victorious! Never give up on your dreams.

Tip of the Day: Pray, plan, prepare, and prosper.

Prayer: *Lord,* sometimes I feel stuck and like I am going in circles. I know You have more in store for me. Help me to seek Your will for my life through prayer. Help me to learn from my experiences. I look forward to a future of hope that is good and rich with new experiences. May the old things pass away as I embrace the new things You bring into my life. Today, I commit to living out the dreams and visions that You have placed inside of me. I will pray over everything I do and give You thanks in all things. In Jesus's name I pray. Amen.

....

....

....

....

....

....

....

....

....

....

....

....

....

☙ DAY 7 ❧

New Mercies Each Day

Through the Lord's mercies we are not consumed,
Because His compassions fail not.
They are new every morning;
Great *is* Your faithfulness.
(Lamentations 3:22–23)

When I think of the Lord's mercy, compassion, and faithfulness, I am reminded of the hymn, "Great Is Thy Faithfulness" by William M. Runyan. The chorus says:

Great is Thy faithfulness!
Great is Thy faithfulness!
Morning by morning new mercies I see.
All I have needed Thy hand hath provided;
Great is Thy faithfulness, Lord, unto me!

Mercy is showing compassion and forbearance toward an offender.

Forbearance is showing leniency, refraining from the enforcement of something (as a debt, punishment, right, or obligation).

Isn't it nice to know that we serve a God who loves us so much that, even in our disobedience, He extends His love, compassion, mercies, and forbearance to us?

God often withholds the very punishment we rightfully deserve for the sins and offenses we commit against Him. Just take a moment to think about that. Oh, what love and unselfishness these acts of love and kindness display. In Matthew 6:12, Jesus told us to pray, "Forgive us our debts as we forgive our debtors!" Today, call to mind anyone who has offended, hurt, or violated you in any way. Make a list of those you need to forgive. Ask God to touch your heart and mind and help you to forgive as He has forgiven you. Ask Him to help you extend mercy to those on your list just as He has extended mercy and forbearance to you. This may not be easy, but it is necessary for true forgiveness, healing, growth, and abundant blessings.

No matter what has happened or what we have done in this life, God remains faithful to us. He has provided all we need. His mercies toward us are new every morning. We are blessed to have such a loving Father! Let's extend the same lovingkindness to one another.

Tip of the Day: Extend the gift of forgiveness and mercy to someone today. You and that person will be blessed by your act of love.

Prayer: *Lord*, thank You for Your love, kindness, and faithfulness in my life. Help me to forgive others and extend mercy toward them as You have for me. Thanks for all that You have and continue to provide for me. In Jesus's name I pray. Amen.

....

....

....

....

....

....

....

....

....

....

....

....

....

....

....

....

....

....

....

....

....

Trustworthy Guidance

Trust in the Lord with all your heart,
And lean not to our own understanding;
In all your ways acknowledge Him,
And He shall direct your paths.
(Proverbs 3:5–6)

Have you ever found it difficult to make a decision? Have you ever wondered why certain things were happening in your life or in the world today? Many of us have struggled with questions such as these. When we don't know which way to go or what to do or wonder why things are happening, looking to God is more important than ever. In these moments, we have a trustworthy friend who wants to guide us on our journey and help us discover which way to go and what to do.

All we need to do is pray and ask God for His direction. Once we have, we can trust God with the details instead of our own understanding of what is happening. When doubts come, we acknowledge that He's in control—that He is the One directing our path. It is important that we listen, obey, and follow His lead. In doing so, we will experience great peace and find ourselves right in the center of God's will for us.

Tip of the Day: Trust and obey God. Leave all of the consequences of doing that up to Him.

Prayer: *Lord,* when I can't find my way, help me to see Your way. I am asking for Your guidance and direction. When I don't understand what's going on, help me to trust You. Lead me on the right path for my life. In Jesus's name I pray. Amen.

....

....

....

....

....

....

....

....

....

....

....

....

....

....

....

....

....

....

....

....

....

....

....

....

....

....

....

❦ DAY 9 ❧

Present Help When You Need It

God *is* our refuge and strength,
A very present help in trouble.
(Psalm 46:1)

Have you ever experienced a time when you were in desperate need of help but could not find it? Sometimes the storms of life lead us to tough places where we need assistance and strength to make it through. It's so good to know that, in the midst of it all, God is our sure footing. In perilous times such as these, God is our comfort and aid. He promised to never leave us nor forsake us. Indeed, He is a very present help in the time of trouble.

Tip of the Day: Whatever you are going through to-day, know that God is standing by waiting to assist you in your time of trouble.

Prayer: *Lord*, I feel troubled on every side. I am asking for Your help. Come to my aid and rescue me. You and You alone are my strong tower. I take refuge in You. Teach me how to trust You more each day. I pray this In Jesus's name. Amen.

....

....

....

....

....

....

....

....

....

....

....

....

....

....

....

....

....

....

....

....

....

....

....

....

....

....

....

....

....

....

....

....

....

....

More Than a Conqueror

Yet in all these things we are more than conquerors through Him who loved us. (Romans 8:37)

Sometimes we worry about how things will work out with us, our children or family, our bosses, or circumstances that trouble us throughout the day. During those times, it is important to remember how much God loves us. He cares about every little detail of our lives.

As you go throughout the day, I encourage you to walk in the assurance that God is with you. Remember that your day has been ordered by Him. God has already worked out the details of everything that concerns you. Nothing catches God by surprise, nor is anything impossible with Him. When we learn to quiet ourselves, "be still," and allow God to lead us, He teaches us how to walk confidently, knowing we are more than conquerors! My prayer is that you have a victorious day through Christ Jesus, the lover of your soul. May He strengthen you and see you to a victorious end.

Tip of the Day: Today, you can conquer all things with the Lord's help.

Prayer: *Lord*, I thank You for this beautiful day You have made. I choose to rejoice and be glad in it. I cast all my cares upon You because I know You care for me. By faith, I believe I can conquer anything that comes my way, with Your help. In You, I am victorious. In Jesus's name I pray. Amen!

....

....

....

....

....

....

....

....

....

....

....

....

....

....

....

....

....

....

....

....

....

....

....

....

....

....

....

....

....

....

....

....

....

❦ DAY 11 ❧

A Trustworthy Friend

As iron sharpens iron, So a man sharpens the countenance of his friend. (Proverbs 27:17)

My parents often reminded me to carefully consider the company I kept. Close association can certainly bring on assimilation. We become more like the people we spend most of our time with. So we must always be mindful of whom we allow into our most intimate spaces or circles. The company we keep is vital to our present and our future. There is a mental sharpness that comes from good company. We should enhance the lives of our associates, and our friends should enhance our lives. It's important to have the right people in our lives who will challenge us and help us to unearth the creativity God has put in us.

Proverbs 27:17 reminds us that we sharpen the countenance of our friends. Stop for a moment and think about the following questions:

1) Who are your closest friends?
2) What words are they speaking into your life?
3) What are they encouraging you to do?
4) What are they encouraging you to say?
5) What are they encouraging you to watch?
6) What are they encouraging you to eat?
7) Who are they encouraging you to be?

Today, examine whom you are spending most of your time with. Pay attention to what they are pouring into you and how they are impacting your life. Think about what kind of friend you are to others and what type of impact you are making in and on their lives. Ask God to help you be a friend to those in need, and to be an even better friend to the ones you have right now.

Remember, God is a friend you can trust wholeheartedly. His Word helps to grow you. What better friend to sharpen your countenance than your heavenly Father? He will have the greatest, most positive and amazing impact on your life.

Tip of the Day: Choose your friends and company wisely.

Prayer: *God,* thank You for always being my friend. Help me to be a friend to those who need one today. Lord, heighten my discernment to know whom I should spend time with and whom I should not. Help me to be a blessing to those I encounter and who call me friend. May Your Word be a lamp unto our feet and a light unto our paths. In Jesus's name I pray this. Amen.

....

....

....

....

....

....

....

....

....

....

....

....

....

....

....

....

....

....

....

....

....

....

....

....

❦ DAY 12 ❧

Matters of the Heart

The king's heart *is* in the hand of the Lord,
Like the rivers of water;
He turns it wherever He wishes.
(Proverbs 21:1)

Have you ever dealt with an individual who prioritized a process over people or constantly tried to control others with their positional power? Have you had a conversation with someone who said one thing but did the opposite? Maybe someone tried to control you through intimidation and fear tactics.

While we are to respect others, we do not need to fear them. The heart of a person is in God's hand. The next time you encounter someone who tries to control you or others, remember that your response to their actions or attitude will predict your outcome. "A soft answer turns away wrath" (Proverbs 15:1), but sometimes we also need to carry our people problems to God in prayer.

Instead of arguing with a difficult person or trying to prove your point, pray for the individual as well as yourself. Pray that God will change their heart and guide yours. Your outcome will be blessed when you entrust the situation and the person involved to the Lord. Remind yourself that, yes, God has control over this situation too. May God bless and keep you!

Tip of the Day: When you encounter difficult people, ask God to change their hearts and your heart.

Prayer: *Lord*, Your Word says the king's heart is in Your hands. Help me to be steadfast and immovable as You mold me into the person you want me to be and do the same for all your children. I trust You with my heart. I depend on You, Lord. In Jesus's name I pray. Amen.

....

....

....

....

....

....

....

....

....

....

....

....

....

....

....

....

....

....

....

....

....

....

....

....

....

....

....

☙ DAY 13 ❧

Focus on Good Things

Finally, brethren, whatever things are true, whatever things *are* noble, whatever things *are* just, whatever things *are* pure, whatever things *are* lovely, whatever things *are* of good report, if *there is* any virtue and if *there is* anything praiseworthy—meditate on these things. The things which you learned and received and heard and saw in me, these do, and the God of peace will be with you. (Philippians 4:8–9)

Stop and consider what you have been thinking about. Have you been focusing on positive or negative things? Have you allowed disturbing news or the unkind words of others to prohibit you from believing what God has promised in His Word? Philippians 4:8–9 is a great reminder of where our focus should be. It tells us what to fill our minds with when what is happening in our lives or in the world or our interactions with others leave us feeling uneasy and unsettled.

Dwelling on the wrong things can lead us to wrong actions or situations we should not be in. Whatever we think on will eventually show up in our lives—good or bad.

When we switch our focus from what seems to be going wrong to the power of our loving Father and how He has blessed us in the past, we begin to see the shift in our perspective. We see how He has worked for our good. That is why it is so important to focus on God and His Word. It reminds us of the truth in our particular situation or set of circumstances.

I don't know about you, but today I am setting my affections on those things that are true, noble, just, pure, lovely, and of a good report. I am beginning to feel a peace that surpasses understanding right now! I hope you do too.

Focus on the Man with your master plan. The Master's name is Jesus!

Tip of the Day: Today, purpose to set your thoughts on good things. Remember, God is working all things together for your good.

Prayer: *Today, Lord,* help me to shift my focus from negativity to things that are positive, true, noble, just, pure, lovely, peaceable, and of a good report. Grant me the ability to embrace Your peace that surpasses all

understanding and guard my heart and mind. I pray
this in Jesus's name. Amen.

....

....

....

....

....

....

....

....

....

....

....

....

....

....

....

....

....

....

....

....

....

....

....

....

....

⤙ **DAY 14** ⤚

Conquering Temptation

Therefore let him who thinks he stands take heed lest he fall. No temptation has overtaken you except such as is common to man; but God *is* faithful, who will not allow you to be tempted beyond what you are able, but with the temptation will also make the way of escape, that you may be able to bear *it*. (1 Corinthians 10:12–13)

Think of a time when you did something wrong and later asked yourself, "Why did I do that?" When was the last time you found it hard to do the right thing? Everyone deals with temptation. But what do we do in those moments? Sometimes we may call a friend for accountability. Some of us try to exercise self-control on our own. Sometimes, truth be told, we fall for the thing that tempted us.

It is not easy to resist temptation. But with the help of the Holy Spirit and prayer, we can overcome it.

The Word of God tells us if we resist the devil, he will flee from us. In moments of temptation, we can pray and ask God for the power to resist. He will show us a way of escape. If you are struggling with temptation in some area of your life, you don't have to face it alone.

God will give us more discipline and self-control if we ask. When a temptation is hard to resist, it helps to remember that the pain of discipline hurts less than the price of regret. Keep pushing and keep praying. God will see you through these times.

Tip of the Day: In times of temptation, ask God for help. He wants to show you a way of escape.

Prayer: *Lord*, I need a greater measure of Your Spirit to reside in me. Endow me with more love, joy, peace, longsuffering, kindness, goodness, faithfulness, gentleness, and self-control. Help me to resist the devil so he will flee. When I am tempted, remind me of your word and help me to be more like You. In Jesus's name I pray. Amen.

....

....

....

....

....

....

....

....

....

....

....

....

....

....

....

....

....

....

....

....

....

....

....

....

....

Words of Wisdom that Bring Light

The entrance of Your words gives light. It gives understanding to the simple (Psalm 119:130)

When was the last time you needed wisdom and discernment? When have you found yourself in a dilemma, unable to decide what to do? Sometimes we must make major decisions that will have a lasting effect on our lives. In those moments, it is good to search God's Word and apply it to our situations.

Psalm 119:130 calls the Word of God a lamp unto our feet and a light into our path. It leads us into all truth. As you seek God for more understanding concerning any situation or circumstance in your life, His Word will illuminate all areas of darkness and confusion. It will bring light into your situation and life. You can trust Him. He will see you through those moments.

Tip of the Day: Study the Word of God and it will bring light to any situation in your life.

Prayer: *Lord*, I thank You for going before me to make every crooked path straight. I am seeking more understanding for some specific decisions as I study Your Word more. May the Holy Spirit help me to be obedient and live according to Your Word. I know this will guide me into all truth. May Your will be done in my life. In Jesus's name I pray. Amen.

....

....

....

....

....

....

....

....

....

....

....

....

....

....

....

....

....

....

....

....

....

....

....

....

....

....

....

᭥ DAY 16 ᭥

The Power of Forgiveness

And whenever you stand praying, if you have any-thing against anyone, forgive him, that your Father in heaven may also forgive you your trespasses. (Mark 11:25)

What would you do if today was your last day on earth? Who would you tell, "I love you" or "I forgive you"? Who would you ask for forgiveness? Oftentimes we want those who have wronged us, betrayed us, or hurt us to feel the same level of heartache as we did from their actions. Yet, what does our heavenly Father call us to do in His Word? "Forgive us our debts as we forgive our debtors" (Matt. 6:12)

It is important that we embrace the act of forgive-ness. We must ask for the forgiveness of anyone we may have hurt or offended. It is equally important to extend forgiveness to anyone who has hurt us, both knowingly and unknowingly.

I encourage you to choose to extend love and forgiveness to someone who has hurt you and pray for God's blessings upon that person's life.

Join me in trying to walk and act in love. Let's forgive as we want to be forgiven, and do it today instead of putting it off until tomorrow. The next moment is not promised to any of us.

Think of one person you need to forgive. Reach out to that person today and extend forgiveness. Your blessings can be found in your forgiveness. It will also free you up to love more, live more peaceably, and be filled with more joy.

Tip of the Day: Forgive others as God has forgiven you.

Prayer: *Lord*, thank You for extending grace to me. It is sufficient for today and every day of my life. Thank You for Your tender mercies that are new every morning. *Hallelujah*! Help me to forgive others as much and as consistently as You forgive me. In Jesus's name I pray. Amen.

....

....

....

....

....

....

....

....

....

....

....

....

....

....

≈§ **DAY 17** ᖨ∾

The Power of Patience

By your patience possess your souls. (Luke 21:19)

The Google Dictionary *defines patience* as "the capacity to accept or tolerate delay, trouble, or suffering without getting angry or upset" (www.google.com).

Longsuffering is often defined as *love on trial.* It enables us to forbear and forgive others (see Colossians 3:13). As with the other manifestations of spiritual fruit, we can't produce it without the Holy Spirit's help. He gives us the supernatural ability to be patient and longsuffering with joy (see Colossians 1:11).

When you think about your life, in what area can you use more patience?

Patience is a powerful force. In patience we are to possess our souls (see Luke 21:19). The fruit of patience in our lives actually helps us to take control of thoughts, emotions, and responses. Let's pray that God gives us more patience. After all, God extends great patience with us. What if we extend the same to others? Remember, we can't do this alone. We need the Holy Spirit to help us.

Tip of the Day: Think of someone in your life who regularly demonstrates or extends the virtue of patience toward you. Call or send a note to him or her to express your appreciation for this attribute.

Prayer: *Father,* today I ask that You endow me with more of the fruits of Your Holy Spirit. Help me to forgive as well as extend the same patience, grace, and love to others that You extend to me day by day. I pray this in Jesus's name. Amen.

....

....

....

....

....

....

....

....

....

....

....

....

....

....

....

....

....

....

....

....

....

....

....

....

....

....

....

God Will Fight for You

> You will not *need* to fight in this *battle*. Position yourselves, stand still and see the salvation of the Lord, who is with you, O Judah and Jerusalem! Do not fear or be dismayed. (2 Chronicles 20:17)

With God on your side, who can be against you! With God on your side, you have everything you need. Whether it is peace, joy, hope, love, provision, or protection, you can find it in Him.

If you are currently facing a situation that seems insurmountable, or if you're in a battle that seems too hard to bear, know that every battle or obstacle you encounter can be won with God through prayer.

I've experienced many circumstances that seemed too hard to bear, and battles when I wondered, *Lord, how will You work this one out for me?*

I have found that if I acknowledge God's presence in my life and ask Him to help me, He is always available to assist. Even in times when I did not think it was possible for a situation to turn around and work out for the good, He caused me to come out victorious.

Whether it be sickness, grief, trouble on your job, disruption in your home, or troubled relationships, I encourage you to position yourself in prayer. Accept the help that God sends to you and watch Him work things out for your greater good. It may not work out exactly as you want it to, but chances are you will find that the outcome is far better than you expected. 2 Corinthians 2:14 says, "Now Thanks be unto God, which always causeth us to triumph in Christ" (KJV). God will fight your battles when you give them to Him.

Tip of the Day: As you go throughout this day, remember God is with you. No battle is too great for our God! With God on your side, you will always come out victorious.

Prayer: *Lord,* when life becomes unbearable and the battles seem too hard, help me to give my burdens over to You and leave them there. Thank You for caring for me and fighting on my behalf. I know that the weapons of my warfare are not carnal, but they are mighty through You, Lord God, to the pulling down of strongholds. I will trust You in all things, so I claim the victory today. In Jesus's name I pray. Amen.

....

....

....

....

....

....

....

....

....

....

....

....

....

....

....

....

....

....

....

....

....

....

....

....

....

....

....

....

❧ DAY 19 ❧

The Greatest Love

And now abide faith, hope, love, these three; but the greatest of these *is* love. (1 Corinthians 13:13)

When was the last time someone told you, "I love you"? Have you ever had your heart broken by someone you thought loved you? Have you ever had someone say they loved you, yet their actions demonstrated something different? As I pondered these questions, I examined the true definition of love as well as how we receive and extend true love to others.

Wikipedia defines love as "the ultimate expression of God's loyalty, purity, and mercy extended toward His people—to be reflected in human relationships of brotherly/sisterly concern, marital fidelity, and adoration of God" (https://en.wikipedia.org/wiki/Love).

This definition causes me to think about what love really means, how I use the word, and how it has been used with me. It really challenged me to think about how we, as humans, demonstrate God's love through our thoughts, deeds, and actions. When we say we love someone, it should be in the way God intends for us to demonstrate His love. We must ask ourselves if we are a true reflection of His love, or if we have misused or abused the word. Are we guilty of misusing or abusing someone in the name of love? Perhaps we have been manipulated by someone's tainted definition.

Today, let's reflect on the true definition of love and how it is expressed. True love is always a reflection of God, because God is love. Take time to Read 1 Corinthians 13 today. Consider if you are giving as well as receiving the love that the passage speaks of. How can you display the love that the world needs so desperately.

Thank God for showing us *true love*.

Tip of the Day: Receive the love God gives you and share it with others.

Prayer: *Thank You, Lord,* for always loving me and demonstrating what true love is. Forgive me for the times I have failed to show true love to others. Help me to love more like You. In Jesus's name I pray. Amen.

....

....

....

....

....

....

....

....

....

....

....

....

....

INSPIRATION FOR YOUR JOURNEY

⌘ **DAY 20** ⌘

Indecision

If any of you lacks wisdom, let him ask of God, who gives to all liberally and without reproach, and it will be given to him. (James 1:5)

Sometimes when faced with decisions and choices that will have a lasting impact on our lives, we are unsure what to do. Uncertainty or indecisiveness is something we have all experienced at some point in our lives. In those moments, we can ask God to give us divine wisdom to make the right choice or decision. We can also ask for the strength to carry out His instructions, whatever they may be. With the help of the Holy Spirit, we can move forward in faith with the assurance that we are doing the right thing.

Tip of the Day: Before making a move, seek God's wisdom or godly counsel.

Prayer: *Today, Lord,* I ask You to guide me and instruct me in the way I should go. I ask for Your wisdom and the courage to obey Your instructions. Help me not to waver or be double minded in my decisions, but to trust You wholeheartedly, knowing Your Holy Spirit is leading me into truth. Help me to make wise decisions that are pleasing to You and in accordance with Your will for my life. In Jesus's name I pray. Amen.

Indecision

....

....

....

....

....

....

....

....

....

....

....

....

....

....

❦ **DAY 21** ❧

Help Me, Lord

I don't really understand myself, for I want to do what is right, but I don't do it. Instead, I do what I hate. (Romans 7:15 NLT)

Have you *ever been* in a situation when you knew the right thing to do but didn't do it for one reason or another?

There are times in our lives when we know what to do but we just don't do it. We may know God's standards and the kind of activities we should engage in as well as those we should avoid. But do we always follow His commands? It's only by God's grace and with His help that we do what we know we should.

When we are on the brink of faltering or losing our way, God will step in if we cry out for His help. The simple prayer, "Lord, help me," invites His supernatural power to come into any situation we find ourselves in.

Tip of the Day: God is our keeper.

Prayer: *Lord*, strengthen me through Your Holy Spirit. I ask for courage to do what is right. When the world tries to pull me in one direction, Your Spirit is calling me to press on toward the mark of the high calling which is in You. I want all that I do to be pleasing in Your sight. You are my strong tower, and I run to You for safety. I trust You with my life, and I thank You for strengthening me in moments when I am weak. Thank You for being my present help in my time of need. In Jesus's name I pray. Amen.

....

....

....

....

....

....

....

....

....

....

....

....

....

....

....

....

....

....

....

....

....

....

....

....

....

....

....

....

O Ye of Little Faith

So Jesus said to them, "Because of your unbelief;
for assuredly, I say to you, if you have faith as a
mustard seed, you will say to this mountain, 'Move
from here to there,' and it will move; and nothing
will be impossible for you." (Matthew 17:20)

When was the last time you thought about how
you handle life's challenges? What coping mechanism
do you rely on? When life gets tough, what do you revert to that feels safe and comfortable? Do you become
reclusive, revert back to what your upbringing taught
you, or revert back to what you used to do? If you are
like me, you've discovered that the old way may not
necessarily be the best way to handle a situation.

Instead of reverting back to what is comfortable
and familiar, it helps to remember God's Word. If we
have faith in God, we can speak to any giant or anything that presses against us. We can command it to

be moved out of our way! Nothing is impossible with God. He will make a way for us. Whenever we put our faith into action, God can see us through.

Being a person of faith doesn't mean that we won't question things or go through tough times. Faith doesn't keep us from facing challenges along life's journey. It just means we have more opportunities to learn to lean on God and depend on Him. He will indeed help us. God's help may not always come in the way or form that we want it, but if we allow Him to work, it will be what is best for us.

Tip of the Day: A little bit of faith goes a long way.

Prayer: *Lord*, when I am in doubt, increase my faith. When things seem insurmountable, increase my faith. When the going gets rough, increase my faith. Help me to trust You more. Help me to have mustard seed faith. I pray all this in Jesus's name. Amen.

....

....

....

....

....

....

....

....

....

....

....

....

....

....

How Do I Hear His Voice?

Then He said, "Go out, and stand on the mountain before the Lord." And behold, the Lord passed by, and a great and strong wind tore into the mountains and broke the rocks in pieces before the Lord, *but* the Lord *was* not in the wind; and after the wind an earthquake, *but* the Lord *was* not in the earthquake; and after the earthquake a fire, *but* the Lord *was* not in the fire; and after the fire a still small voice. (1 Kings 19:11–12)

Perhaps someone told you to "listen for the still, small voice of God," but you felt as though you couldn't hear His voice or see Him working in your life. Well, you are not alone.

Life seems to be moving at a faster pace by the day. Sometimes our problems or current situations scream so loudly that we can't hear anything else. Mental stress fogs our judgment while the internet, television, cell phones, and text messages compete for our time. No wonder we can't hear that still, small voice. Sometimes we ignore that feeling in our gut or the intuition that prompts us in a certain direction. That is the still, small voice of God speaking to us. The Word tells us that God's sheep hear His voice and the voice of a stranger we will not follow. (See John 10:27.)

I encourage you to take a few minutes out of each day to be quiet. Turn off the TV, walk away from the computer, put down that phone, and turn off your music. Be still and commune with God. You may be surprised by what you hear and how you notice Him working in your life.

Tip of the Day: Take five to ten minutes today to be still and pay attention to how spending time with God changes your perspective on specific situations in your life as well as in the world.

Prayer: *Father,* help me to be still and listen more attentively for Your voice. Many things are competing for my time with You. Help me to eliminate any unnecessary clutter or chatter in my life and find that quiet place to commune. I want to hear Your voice more clearly than anything else in my life. In Jesus's name I pray. Amen.

....

....

....

....

....

....

....

....

....

....

....

....

....

....

....

....

....

....

....

....

....

....

....

....

....

....

❧ DAY 24 ❧

Comfort for the Brokenhearted

The Lord is close to the brokenhearted;
he rescues those whose spirits are crushed.
(Psalm 34:18 NLT)

I lost my mother in 2014. At times, the grief seemed
unbearable. Whenever I felt overwhelmed with grief, I
asked the Lord for strength to make it through the day.

Over time, I resolved within myself to not allow
grief to steal my joy. When I was weak, I asked God to
allow His strength to be made perfect in me.

As you deal with the loss of someone or something you love, I encourage you to ask the Lord to send
someone your way who can help in your time of need.
You may come across a friend, a complete stranger, a
professional counselor, or a grief recovery program that
can assist you. I encourage you to accept the help God

provides. The Holy Spirit is there to guide you as well. You don't have to walk through your darkest hours and times of grief alone. Be encouraged! Know that others have gone through the grieving process and you can too. God is always with you to give you strength.

Tip of the Day: Today, whenever you feel grieved in your spirit, say a quick prayer asking God to strengthen you and to send the help you need.

Prayer: *Lord*, You are my strength; You are my refuge and my fortress. You are my very present help in time of need. Lord, strengthen me and comfort my grieving heart. Lord, I need You more than ever right now. I trust You to heal my heart and help me to move on to a brighter day. In Jesus's name I pray. Amen.

....

....

....

....

....

....

....

....

....

....

....

....

....

INSPIRATION FOR YOUR JOURNEY

❦ DAY 25 ❧

My Good Days Outweigh My Bad Days

Bless the Lord, O my soul;
And all that is within me, *bless* His holy name!
Bless the Lord, O my soul,
And forget not all His benefits.
(Psalm 103:1–2)

Sometimes we allow the situations we face to cloud our memory of the many blessings God has bestowed upon us. God is a good God. He has done great things for His children, including us.

Psalm 103:1 can help us remember God's goodness. Whenever we stop and take time to reflect on all that the Lord has done, it should cause us to praise and bless His glorious name. This is something we can practice every day of our lives, being mindful of what He has already done. God has forgiven all of our iniquities. He has healed us of all diseases. He has redeemed our lives from destruction. Hallelujah! God crowns us each day with His lovingkindness and tender mercies. We recognize and receive many benefits when we are in a close relationship with the Lord.

Tip of the Day: Spend time today thanking God for all of His goodness and the benefits that He has bestowed upon you. You will find yourself blessing His holy name.

Prayer: *Lord*, may these words permeate my soul. Bless the Lord, O my soul and all that is within me. I bless Your holy name! May I remember all of the priceless benefits that come from knowing You. Thank You, Lord, for blessing me. In Jesus's name I pray. Amen.

....

....

....

....

....

....

....

....

....

....

....

....

....

....

⤬ DAY 26 ⤬

Pray about Everything

For the weapons of our warfare *are* not carnal but mighty in God for pulling down strongholds. (2 Corinthians 10:4)

Everything you need from God can be obtained in prayer: discernment, direction, abundance, His *provision*, His strategies . . . anything. You fill in blank with what you need.

Every battle and obstacle that you encounter can be won and overcome through prayer.

Remember the Serenity Prayer this week: *God, grant me the serenity to accept the things I cannot change; courage to change the things I can; and wisdom to know the difference.*

Don't just pray for yourself but pray for others this week as well. Watch God work a miracle in your life as you do.

Tip of the Day: Remember, God is standing by waiting on you to commune with Him. Prayer changes things.

Prayer: *Lord*, please remind me today that every obstacle and challenge I might experience can be overcome through prayer. In moments of difficulty, help me to quiet myself, say a prayer, and listen for Your answer before moving forward. In Jesus's name I pray. Amen.

....

....

....

....

....

....

....

....

....

....

....

....

....

Don't Be Dismayed— He Will Instruct You

I will instruct you and teach you in the way you should go; I will guide you with My eye.
(Psalm 32:8)

When life gets tough, don't give up. Press through, push through, and pray through. You can get through it! Whatever you are called to, know that you can do it. You can because you are the only one called to your particular assignment. When doubts come, trust and believe that God will guide you and provide you with all of the instructions, guidance, and resources you need.

When you feel you have lost your way or your momentum, pray and ask God for instructions. He will give them to you liberally and will not withhold what you need. Have no fear! Change is on the horizon. God is on your side. All things are possible for those who believe. Trust Him to show you the way.

Tip of the Day: Ask for direction and you will receive it.

Prayer: *Lord,* I ask for Your guidance and direction. Help me to know Your ways and honor them. Help me as I press, push, and pray through every situation. I trust You to direct my path and protect me on my journey. Thank You, Lord! I pray in Jesus's name. Amen.

....

....

....

....

....

....

....

....

....

....

....

....

....

....

....

....

....

....

....

....

....

....

....

....

....

....

....

....

....

....

....

....

....

Have Faith in God

So Jesus answered and said to them, "Have faith in
God." (Mark 11:22)

God is not complicated, but we have a tendency to
complicate things. As you approach this day, no matter what you may be facing, be determined to obey Jesus's words and have faith in God. Remember, without
faith it is impossible to please Him. Seek the Master
in all things today, for He is a rewarder of those who
diligently seek Him. God's blessings may come in pe-
culiar ways, so keep your eyes and ears open to Him.
Be expectant that God will give you His best. I simply
encourage you to trust Him.

Tip of the Day: Keep the faith!

Prayer: *Lord,* increase my faith. Help my unbelief.
Help me to trust You when I cannot see my way. Help

me to know that I can do all things through Christ who strengthens me. I am asking You to help me to move in the direction You would have me to go. I will trust You on my life's journey. I pray in Jesus's name. Amen.

....

....

....

....

....

....

....

....

....

....

....

....

....

....

Be Still

Be still, and know that I *am* God.
(Psalm 46:10)

When life feels like it is caving in on you, it is important to be still, listen for the voice of God, and seek His direction. Taking time to be still before God, praying, listening, and being obedient to whatever He says makes it possible for Him to show up and work things out on our behalf.

Most of the time, we want results in our timing. We might believe if we just had a husband or a wife, bought a new car or house, had a different job or more money, we would be happier and have a better life. We tend to get impatient and attempt to make things happen for ourselves, but when we exhaust our human efforts we realize how much we need God.

What would happen if we made a decision to go after more of God instead of more of what we want?

We need more of His Spirit infused throughout our being—in our thoughts, our hearing, our sight, our taste, and what we touch. We can never go wrong with more of God, but more times than not, we will certainly go wrong without Him.

When the storms of life shake your world, I encourage you to allow the Holy Spirit to comfort you and give you guidance on how to progress. Just "be still" in the moment.

Today, spend some quiet time with God. Take a few minutes each day and accept the invitation for Him to take you away from your trials and the storms of life. God is waiting and wanting to work everything out for your good. Why don't you let Him? Try to relax, trust Him more, and know that He is God of every situation.

Tip of the Day: Be still and let God work on your behalf. You won't regret it.

Prayer: *Lord,* when I am anxious, lead me to the rock that is stronger than I. When I can't see my way through, help me to slow down and listen for Your voice. It is my desire to walk with You, Lord. Help me to be still and know that You are the God of every situation and circumstance in my life. In Jesus's name I pray. Amen.

The Purpose of Pruning

Rest in the LORD, and wait patiently for Him.
(Psalm 37:7)

Resting in the Lord and waiting patiently for Him is not an easy thing to accomplish. When God leads us into a season of resting and waiting upon Him, He often uses the time to do a specific work in our lives.

Waiting is the greatest pruning process. In gardening terms, pruning is the practice of the selective removal of parts of a plant. It is used to remove dead wood, shape (control and direct growth), improve or maintain a plant's health, and to reduce the risk of falling branches. Pruning is also used for both harvesting and increasing the yield or quality of flowers and fruit. The practice entails *targeted* removal of diseased, damaged, dead, non-productive, structurally unsound, or otherwise unwanted tissue from crops and landscaped plants. Specialized pruning practices may be applied to certain plants.

The key thing in pruning is this: It is important that the plant or tree limbs are kept intact during the process, as this is what helps keep the plant or tree in an upright position. Pruning trees and plants parallels God's pruning process in our lives. As children of God, we are like beautiful flowers and trees in His garden of life. We are here on earth to continue to illuminate His beauty as well as to produce the fruit of His Spirit. We are here to edify His kingdom as people made in His image.

There are times when He has to remove or cut back what doesn't belong in our lives. This includes people who do not add to what He has called us to do. God has to cut back things, behaviors, strongholds, and traits that may deter us from His call on our lives or keep us from our purpose and destiny.

The pruning process is not fun, nor does it feel good, but it is indeed necessary. We can be grateful that God loves us enough to prune us whenever necessary and keep us intact throughout the process. Pruning may look awkward and feel strange to us, but God doesn't allow others to see what we are going through. What looks a little ugly to us for a short time, will always yield greater beauty on the other side.

I encourage you to have faith that God knows all, sees all, and is in control of everything. We can rest in the fact that God is working everything together for our good as we wait on Him. It is after the pruning process that we can flourish and be all God has called us to be!

Tip of the day: God's pruning process does not always feel good to you, but it is good for you. Let His pruning yield new fruit in your life.

Prayer: *God*, thank You for the pruning process. Help me to accept Your will for my life. I know it is for my betterment. Your love and tender care make me better. I thank You for pruning that leads me to my passion, reminds me of the vision that You put in me, and helps me to fulfill my God ordained purpose on this earth! In all things, I will give You praise. In Jesus's name I pray. Amen.

....

....

....

....

....

....

....

....

....

....

....

....

....

....

....

....

❦ DAY 31 ❦

Don't Forfeit Perfect Peace

You will keep in perfect *and* constant peace *the one* whose mind is steadfast [that is, committed and focused on You—in both inclination and character], Because he trusts *and* takes refuge in You [with hope and confident expectation]. (Isaiah 26:3 AMP)

God promises to keep us in perfect peace when our minds stay on Him. Many times we allow the cares of the world and our personal circumstances to be our focal points. Situations like trying to find our next job, trouble with our current employment, difficult bosses, troubled relationships, divorce, financial challenges, and troubled children can be worrisome. However, God promised to carry our burdens for us if we pray and place them in His hands.

Don't forfeit God's peace today. Remember to keep your mind on Him and not your circumstances. That will give you peace!

Today, remember the words of the famous song, "What a Friend We Have in Jesus!" by Alan Jackson.

What a friend we have in Jesus,
All our sins and grief to bear!
What a privilege to carry
Everything to God in prayer!

Oh, what peace we often forfeit,
Oh, what needless pain we bear,
All because we do not carry
Everything to God in prayer.

Tip of the Day: Focus on what God says about your situation.

Prayer: *Lord*, I am grateful that You are my rock and my comforter. When situations are too much for me to bear, help me to remember that You are with me. Lord, You are here to help, guide, and comfort me. Let my mind focus on Your goodness and all that You have brought me through. May my mind be placed at ease and peace as I keep it focused on You, Lord. In Jesus's name I pray this. Amen.

....

....

....

....

....

....

....

....

....

....

....

....

....

Where Do You Place Your Trust?

Some *trust* in chariots and some in horses; but we will remember the name of the Lord our God.
(Psalm 20:7)

Some of us put our trust in our jobs, our money, other people, or even the world's system, when we really should be mindful to be more trusting in God. Some other methods and people we have trusted have failed us miserably. However, no matter what is going on in our lives or in the world around us, we can trust the Lord in all things. Psalm 20:7 says, "Some trust in chariots and some in horses; but we will remember the name of the Lord our God."

We benefit from always being mindful of who He is. God is our strong tower because we can run to Him for safety. He is our buckler and our shield. He is our provider. He is our peace and quiet in the midst of every storm. He is our joy, which the world did not give and cannot take away. He is Emmanuel, God with us. He is truth. He is our Redeemer. He is our *everything*! We can put our trust in Him for anything. When you ponder that thought, you may come to realized that He has never failed you yet. If that does not make you leap for joy, I don't know what will!

Tip of the Day: Trust in Him. He will never leave you nor forsake you.

Prayer: *Lord*, Your name is a strong tower. I can always run to You and find safety. Remind me to always trust in You, Lord, as You are my surety and the answer to all of my needs. In Jesus's name I pray. Amen.

❧ **DAY 33** ❧

The Process

For the vision *is* yet for an appointed time;
But at the end it will speak, and it will not lie.
Though it tarries, wait for it;
Because it will surely come,
It will not tarry.
(Habakkuk 2:3)

Have you ever wondered why God's promises take so long to manifest? God has many blessings in store for us, but He also has a specific timetable for them to come to pass. If we get ahead of God's timing, we can mess things up. He often uses the time of waiting to set details in perfect order for us—for our destiny and future.

The time of waiting is required to accomplish His purpose in our lives. It's like the process of the caterpillar turning into a butterfly. If we break the cocoon open before the complete process of metamorphosis takes place, the caterpillar will not become the butterfly. It may struggle to break through that cocoon, but only after its struggle can it be released to fly.

Funny that a butterfly seems so fragile, yet it possessed the strength to break through a hard cocoon without being injured. Isn't God amazing? The butterfly can endure the struggle because it has gone through the metamorphosis, waited for the appointed time to be released, and operated in divine order.

Like butterflies, we need to allow God's process to work in our lives. But sometimes we delay the timetable when we don't go through it the way God instructs us to. While we are waiting for the fulfillment of our vision and dreams, it helps to ask God to sustain us with grace. When He moves on our behalf, we will have a greater appreciation for the delay. We will understand the reason for the wait and thank God for it. The manifestation of the promise will be well worth the wait.

Tip of the Day: What God has for you is worth waiting for. Though it tarries, wait for it.

Prayer: *Lord*, I pray that You will help my unbelief. Your Word says that though the vision and the dream tarries, wait for it. Help me to have more patience, endurance, and perseverance, and to walk in obedience. Help me to trust You more, knowing that You are working things together for my good during the wait. Thank You, in advance, for the fulfillment and manifestation of my dreams and vision. In Jesus's name I pray. Amen.

....

....

....

....

....

....

....

....

....

....

....

....

....

....

....

....

....

....

....

....

....

....

....

....

✴ DAY 34 ✴

Good Shepherd

The Lord *is* my shepherd; I shall not want. He makes me to lie down in green pastures;
He leads me beside the still waters. He restores my soul; He leads me in the paths of righteousness for His name's sake.
(Psalm 23:1–3)

We, like sheep, are dependent on a shepherd to lead, guide, provide for, and protect us. When we are wise enough to follow God, the Good Shepherd, He will lead us to the right people, places, and things. We can have a sense of peace when we allow Him to lead. However, we cannot blame God for the lack of peace and the troubled environment we create for ourselves when we go our own way.

God knows how to place us in the plush green pastures and lead us by the still, peaceful waters of life to restore our souls. Imagine that! We only reach these places by obediently following His leading. Rebellion against His leading is really rebellion against our own best interest. Keep this in mind the next time you are tempted to do things your way or instead of God's way.

Tip of the Day: There is safety in trusting God's leading.

Prayer: *Lord,* thank You for being my Good Shepherd. With You, Lord, I have everything I need. Help me to obediently follow Your leading as You reveal Your will for my life. As I follow You, surely goodness shall follow me. I pray that Your Holy Spirit will dwell within me and guide me forever and ever. I pray all this in Jesus's name. Amen.

A New Dawning

I will go before you
And make the crooked places straight;
I will break in pieces the gates of bronze
And cut the bars of iron.
(Isaiah 45:2)

Think of a time when you were so excited that you felt like you could burst at your seams. Do you sense right now that it's your time—that your due season has come? Do you have faith that it can happen? Perhaps the time is near. Now is not the time to get distracted or off track. This is the time to dust off that business plan, to start preparing for the wonderful relationship you so desire, or to pursue your passion and purpose.

Sense that positive energy now. You can be encouraged as well as inspired to move forward knowing that God has promised to go before you and make your path straight. He promises to go before us and remove or guide us through any obstacle that might deter us from what He has in store for us. So fret not, for the Lord is with you to guide and deliver you into your season of breakthrough.

Just be obedient to what God tells you to do. There is greatness in your future!

Tip of the Day: Your due season is here. Rejoice with thanksgiving!

Prayer: *Lord*, my confidence resides in You. I know the race is not given to the swift or the strong but to the one who endures until the end. I trust You to go before me and lead me in the way I should go. I trust You, Lord, to make a way out of no way and to manifest all that You have placed inside of me to be delivered here on earth. My season has come! I believe it and I receive it now. This is my prayer. In Jesus's name I pray. Amen.

....

....

....

....

....

....

....

....

....

....

....

....

....

....

....

....

....

Just Light Afflictions

For our light affliction, which is but for a moment,
is working for us a far more exceeding *and* eternal
weight of glory. (2 Corinthians 4:17)

You might have heard the saying, "Trouble doesn't
last always." It's true that trouble doesn't last forever, but
have you ever felt like your current situation was taking
way too long to change for the better? Have you asked,
God, when will this be over? Or maybe you've said to
yourself, *If one more person tells me that my breakthrough
is right around the corner, I am going to scream!*

Well, you are not alone. The beautiful thing is that
God really does have the final say in all of our affairs.
He really does have everything pertaining to us under
control. You might be right on the cusp of receiving
your breakthrough. Just don't give up. What you are
going through is temporary.

Second Corinthians 4:17–18 in The Message Bible says,

> So we're not giving up. How could we! Even though on the outside it often looks like things are falling apart on us, on the inside, where God is making new life, not a day goes by without his unfolding grace. These hard times are small potatoes compared to the coming good times, the lavish celebration prepared for us. There's far more here than meets the eye. The things we see now are here today, gone tomorrow. But the things we can't see now will last forever.

In times of challenges, pain, and uncertainty, this continues to bring me encouragement and courage to keep walking with the Lord and trusting Him. I pray it does the same for you.

Tip of the Day: Don't give up. What you are going through is temporary.

Prayer: *Lord*, help me to remember that the light afflictions I deal with daily will end. Help me to keep my eyes on the prize of the high calling that is in You, Lord. In Jesus's name I pray. Amen.

....

....

....

....

....

....

....

....

....

....

....

....

....

....

❦ DAY 37 ❧

Pain, Process, Purpose

Resist him, steadfast in the faith, knowing that the same sufferings are experienced by your brotherhood in the world. But may the God of all grace, who called us to His eternal glory by Christ Jesus, after you have suffered a while, perfect, establish, strengthen, and settle *you*. To Him *be* the glory and the dominion forever and ever. Amen. (1 Peter 5:9–11)

There are times in our lives when we feel as though we are in a storm or experiencing something that no one else has suffered. It may even seem like no one could possibly know or understand what we are going through or how we feel at the moment. We feel like what we are going through will last forever. We must remember, however, that storms don't last forever no matter how bad they are or how long they seem to linger. This applies to both the spiritual and the natural realm.

I have learned from experience that pain often pushes us to depend more on God. Valuable lessons have come through the pain and storms of life, when I've slowed down, quieted myself, and paid close attention to what God desired to teach me. If a storm doesn't kill us, which it typically doesn't, oftentimes we discover that we are stronger than we realized. We develop an even greater degree of strength simply by enduring the storm. I have found this to be true in my life. Perhaps you have as well.

God promises that He will never leave us nor forsake us. He promises to make His strength perfect in our lives during times of weakness. We can learn several things from this passage of Scripture: First, God asks us to have faith and remain steadfast in our faith. Second, others are experiencing some of the same things as us, so we are not alone. Third, God's grace is enough to get us through any storm. Fourth, after we have suffered a while, God perfects, establishes, strengthens, and settles us. And last, all glory belongs to God because He has dominion and power over everything including the very storm we may be facing right now. Isn't that encouraging?

When you experience pain, be willing to go through the entire process, no matter how long or short it may last. It has the potential to lead you into your purpose. Victory awaits you on the other end of the storm.

Tip of the Day: God is always on your side and by your side!

Prayer: *Lord,* I put my faith and trust in You. Thank You for watching over me, perfecting those things that concern me, and establishing and strengthening me. Thank You for settling every matter that pertains to my life. In Jesus's name I pray. Amen.

....

....

....

....

....

....

....

....

....

....

....

....

....

....

....

....

....

....

....

....

❧ DAY 38 ☙

Moving Forward after Loss

Blessed *are* those who mourn,
For they shall be comforted. (Matthew 5:4)

Have you ever had a difficult time moving on after the loss of someone close to you? Remember the love you have shared. The bond created between you, God, and your loved one can never be broken even in death.

Even though your loved one is physically no longer with you, you may still feel a bond with them. You may wonder how this is possible. It is because of the pure bond of love that God placed in our hearts for others. It defies the natural realm and gives us a tiny glimpse of His love for us all.

Whenever you are in a time of grieving, ask God to give you strength for each difficult moment. (I have to do this daily.) Though your heart may feel heavy, allow your departed one's history of love and the memories you treasure to envelope you just as God's love does.

Feel and remember it. May it serve to brighten your countenance and lessen your tears.

Tip of the Day: God will help you heal as you process through your loss. Trust Him.

Prayer: *Lord,* my heart aches right now. My heart is heavy, and I am crying out to the Rock that is higher than I, which is You, Lord. Give me strength in this moment to work through the grief. Comfort me and wipe my tears away. I miss them so much. Lord, send Your Holy Spirit to comfort me in this time of heaviness. I thank You for keeping me! In Jesus's name I pray. Amen!

....

....

....

....

....

....

....

....

....

....

....

....

....

....

....

....

....

....

....

....

....

....

....

....

....

Fret Not

Fret not thyself because of evildoers, neither be thou envious against the workers of iniquity. For they shall soon be cut down like the grass, and wither as the green herb.

Trust in the Lord, and do good; so shalt thou dwell in the land, and verily thou shalt be fed. Delight thyself also in the Lord: and he shall give thee the desires of thine heart.

Commit thy way unto the Lord; trust also in him; and he shall bring it to pass.

(Psalm 37:1–5 KJV)

A well-known expression says nice guys (or girls) always finish last. Have you ever felt like those who did wicked things or gloried in their sin seem to always get away with their evil deeds? Has it seemed like you received a more severe punishment than someone else who made the same mistakes?

You may have especially felt this way when wronged by someone you thought loved you and had your best interest at heart. Though people may appear to get away with wrong behavior, they don't. God has promised that evildoers will be brought to justice on the appointed day. Remember that what we experience here on earth is temporary. It does not compare to what will happen in eternity. Today, be determined to set your affection on the things of God and to walk in forgiveness. He has the last say in every matter.

Tip of the Day: Put your trust in God and His way of handling things. You will come out victorious in the end.

Prayer: *Father*, I thank You for the grace and mercy You show me. Help me to always remember that the things of this earth are temporal, and my life's purpose and goal is to seek and do Your will. In the end, when I do things Your way, victory is my assured finish. Thank You. I give You praise. In Jesus's name I pray. Amen.

....

....

....

....

....

....

....

....

....

....

....

....

....

....

....

....

....

....

....

....

....

....

....

....

....

....

....

....

Leave the Past Behind

Behold, the former things have come to pass, And new things I declare; before they spring forth I tell you of them. (Isaiah 42:9)

Have you ever held on to memories of a relationship, difficult job, or bad experience for too long? Did you wonder why you felt stuck? Sometimes we hold on to the past for too long. I have a time or two. We may do this because we are afraid releasing it will feel like a loss. Other times, we struggle to believe that greater things await us on the other side of simply letting go. Or we have a hard time trusting that God has a greater plan for our future and that leaving the past behind liberates us to walk into what He has in store for us.

God promises that former things have passed on and new things are coming. He has a new season for you and me. So walk into it freely, boldly, and confidently, knowing that your best days are ahead of you.

Sometimes simply letting go is the best gift you can give yourself. God's choice blessings for you are likely right on the other side of letting that old thing or the past go.

Tip of the Day: Let go of the old thing and let God give you the new thing. It will be a blessing.

Prayer: *Lord,* I thank You that the old things in my life have passed away, and I can look forward to a future filled with hope and expectations of continued blessings from You. I know the plans You have for me are of peace and not of evil. This gives me great hope. Thanks be to You, Lord, from whom all blessings flow! In Jesus's name I pray this. Amen!

....

....

....

....

....

....

....

....

....

....

....

....

....

....

....

....

....

....

....

....

....

....

....

....

....

....

....

Order Information

REDEMPTION
P R E S S

To order additional copies of this book, please visit
www.redemption-press.com
www.nicoleejohnson.com
Also available on Amazon.com and BarnesandNoble.com
Or by calling toll free 1-844-2REDEEM.

CPSIA information can be obtained
at www.ICGtesting.com
Printed in the USA
FFHW021949220419
51885821-57309FF